Cambridge **Discovery Education**™
▶ **INTERACTIVE READERS**

Series editor: Bob Hastings

WATER
VITAL FOR LIFE

W0099706

A2

Genevieve Kocienda

CAMBRIDGE
UNIVERSITY PRESS

Discovery
EDUCATION™

CAMBRIDGE UNIVERSITY PRESS
Cambridge, New York, Melbourne, Madrid, Cape Town,
Singapore, São Paulo, Delhi, Mexico City

Cambridge University Press
32 Avenue of the Americas, New York, NY 10013-2473, USA

www.cambridge.org
Information on this title: www.cambridge.org/9781107622517

© Cambridge University Press 2014

First published 2014

Printed in Hong Kong, China, by Golden Cup Printing Company Limited

A catalog record for this publication is available from the British Library.

Library of Congress Cataloging-in-Publication Data

Kocienda, G.
  Water : vital for life / Genevieve Kocienda.
    pages cm. -- (Cambridge discovery interactive readers)
  ISBN 978-1-107-62251-7 (pbk. : alk. paper)
  1. Water--Juvenile literature. 2. English language--Textbooks for foreign speakers. 3. Readers
(Elementary) I. Title.

GB662.3.K635 2014
553.7--dc23

                              2013014264

ISBN 978-1-107-62251-7

Additional resources for this publication at www.cambridge.org

Layout services, art direction, book design, and photo research: Q2ABillSMITH GROUP
Editorial services: Hyphen S.A.
Audio production: CityVox, New York
Video production: Q2ABillSMITH GROUP

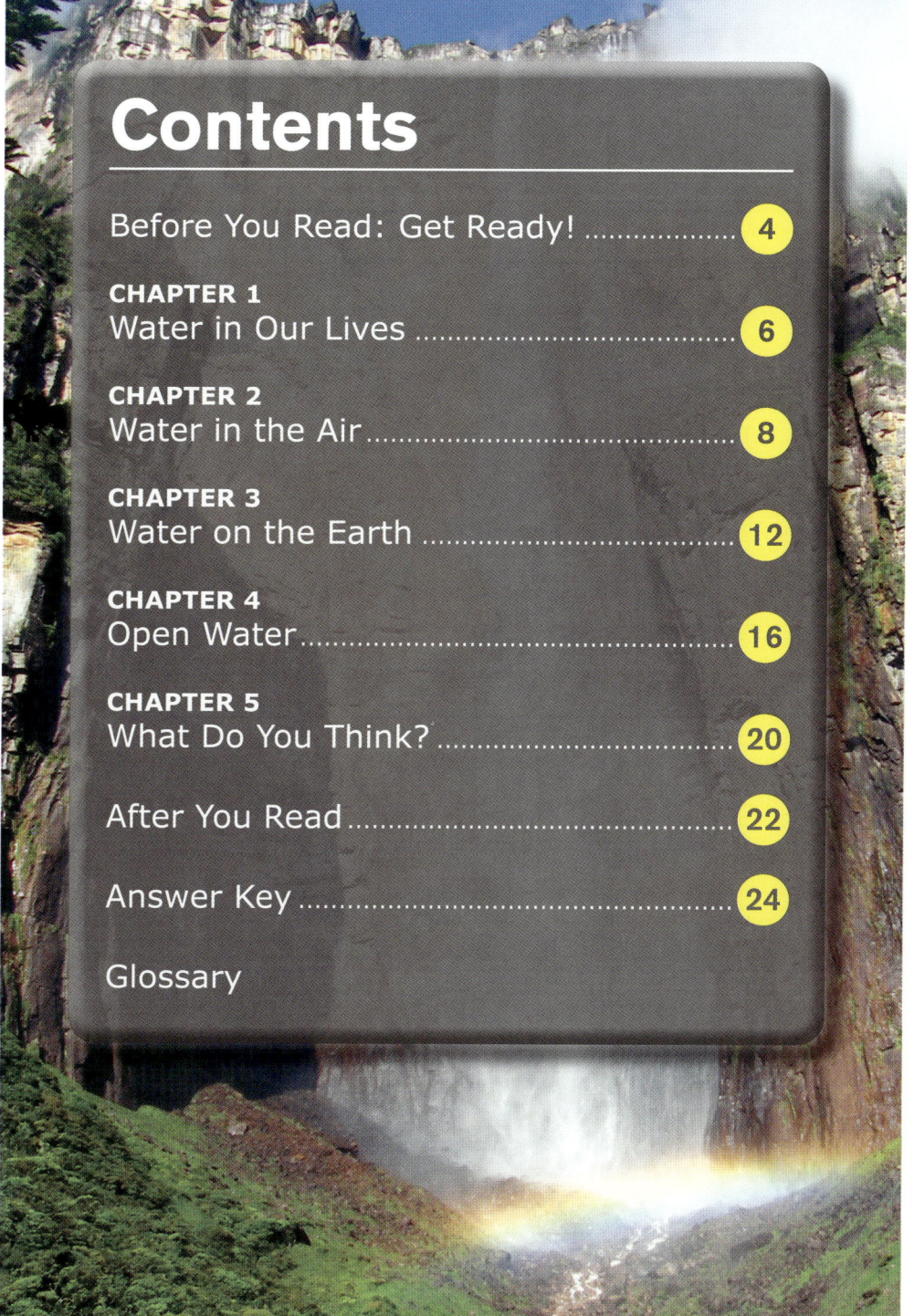

Contents

Before You Read:
Get Ready!

Water is around us and inside of us. Water covers 71 percent of the Earth. Our bodies are about 60 percent water.

Words to Know

Take this quiz about water. Then use the highlighted words to complete the definitions.

❶ How much of the water on Earth is in the oceans?
   a) 55%   b) 75%   c) 97%

❷ At what temperature does water freeze?
   a) 0°C   b) 100°C   c) 1000°C

❸ About how many drops are in one liter of water?
   a) 12,000   b) 20,000   c) 50,000

❹ When a dog comes out of water, it usually shakes water off its body. How much water does a wet dog shake off in four seconds?
   a) 30%   b) 50%   c) 70%   Answers: 1 c, 2 a, 3 b, 4 c

❶ _____: separate pieces of water that fall

❷ _____: when you have water on you; not dry

❸ _____: the large areas of saltwater on the Earth

❹ _____: change from water to ice

Look at the pictures and read the paragraph. Then complete the sentences with the correct highlighted words.

ice (solid)

water (liquid)

steam (gas)

What does water look like? Well, the answer changes with the temperature of the water. Water comes in three forms, or types: solid, liquid, and gas. When water gets very, very cold, it becomes ice. Ice is a solid. It is hard. When the temperature gets warmer, ice melts and becomes water again. Now it is a liquid. When the temperature of water gets very, very hot, it becomes a gas. This is called steam. You can see steam in the air. It looks white.

1. Juice and milk are both examples of a _____.
2. The _____ is how hot or cold something is.
3. When water is a _____, you can feel the heat from the steam.
4. When water is a _____, you can stand on it.
5. You can't stay under the water for a long time. You need to come up to get _____.
6. When you put ice into a warm drink, it _____ quickly.

Video Quest

The Wet Dog Shake

Watch this video to learn how dogs move their bodies to get water off of them.

CHAPTER 1

Water in Our Lives

PEOPLE USE A LOT OF WATER EVERY DAY. HOW MUCH DO YOU USE?

A person can live without food for more than a month. Without water, a person dies in less than one week. We need water inside our bodies.

We need water outside our bodies, too. We need to wash our clothes, our dishes, our food, and our bodies. A person can easily use seven and a half liters of water a day to brush his teeth.

We also need water to make food. It takes three and a half liters of water to process[1] the meat for one hamburger.

[1] **process:** make, change one thing into another

We even need water for the cars we drive. It takes 7,843 liters of water to make four new tires for a car.

Not everyone uses the same amount[2] of water, however. The average person in the United States uses 2,500,000 liters every year. That's the same as an Olympic swimming pool! Someone in China uses about 700,000 liters in a year. People in Uganda or Ethiopia use about 5,000.

One reason for this big difference is the way people use water. Do you leave the water running when you brush your teeth? That's about 11 liters per minute. Do you take a shower or a bath? A five-minute shower uses about 75 liters of water. A full bathtub can hold 130 liters. Do you wash your car in the sunshine, or do you wait until it rains?

[2]**amount:** a lot or a little

Washing cars in sunshine uses more water.

Cumulus clouds

Cirrus clouds

CHAPTER 2

Water in the Air

SOMETIMES WE CAN SEE WATER IN THE AIR – AND SOMETIMES WE CAN'T.

There is a lot of water in the air. Think of clouds, for example. A cloud is a group of very small drops of water. The drops are so small that they float[3] in the air.

There are different kinds of clouds. Cumulus clouds are big and fluffy.[4] Cirrus clouds are very thin and long. When cirrus clouds are in the sky, it means the weather is going to change soon.

Cumulus and cirrus clouds are white. They are white because the drops of water are not very close together. Gray clouds have more water, and the drops are very close together. These are rain clouds, or nimbostratus clouds.

....

[3] **float:** stay in the air or on the top of water
[4] **fluffy:** soft and light

Fog is also a cloud. But it is not up in the sky. It is down on the ground where we walk.

Fog can be beautiful, but it can also be scary.[5] Fog stops you from seeing or hearing things well, so most people don't feel safe when it's very foggy. That's why there is often a lot of fog in scary movies.

Fog in London

London is famous for its fog. In old movies with detectives like Sherlock Holmes, the streets of London are often full of fog. But that wasn't really fog. It was smog!

When fog mixes with smoke in the air, it makes smog. Smog isn't healthy for people to breathe.[6] Today, there isn't as much smog in London as there was in the days of Sherlock Holmes. The air is much cleaner, but it's still often foggy in London.

[5]**scary:** makes you feel afraid or unsafe
[6]**breathe:** take air into your body and let it out again

? APPLY

Look outside. Are there any clouds in the sky? What do they look like? What kind of clouds are they?

When it's humid, your clothes stick to your body.

Humidity means how much water is in the air. On a humid summer day, the skin on your arms, face, and legs feels wet. It's hard to breathe because the air feels heavy. Your clothes stick[7] to your body, and you feel uncomfortable.

When the weather is humid, the **temperature** usually feels higher than it really is. Think about this: when the air temperature is 24°C[8] and there is 0 percent humidity, it feels like 21°C to our bodies. But if the humidity is 100 percent, it feels like 27°C. That's why you feel more comfortable in a warm, dry place than in a warm, humid place.

[7]**stick:** not move freely
[8]**24°C:** pronounced "twenty-four degrees Celsius"

Of course, water can also be in the air in the **form** of rain. When the tiny drops of water in the air come together, they get big and heavy and make clouds. When the drops become too heavy, they fall from the clouds as rain.

If it rains too much rain in one place, then a **flood** can happen. The water from rivers goes onto fields, into towns, and into buildings. But there are good floods and bad floods. Good floods can help farmers. The flood waters can bring new richer soil[9] into the fields. That means it's easier for the farmers to grow crops.

Bad floods can kill people and destroy[10] homes. In October 2011, there was a very bad flood in Thailand. As many as 800 people died, and tens of thousands of people lost their homes.

[9] **soil:** the top part of the ground that plants grow in
[10] **destroy:** break

Crops growing in fields after a flood.

?

EVALUATE

Sometimes flood waters are not good for farmers. What are some possible reasons for this?

A reed boat

CHAPTER 3

Water on the Earth

THERE IS WATER EVERYWHERE ON THE
EARTH. PEOPLE SWIM IN IT, TRAVEL ACROSS
IT, AND TAKE VACATIONS ON IT.

Water is important in human[11] history, and rivers are especially important. They bring water for drinking and for growing food. Towns and cities are very often next to rivers.

Rivers are also important for travel and trade. For example, in the Indus Valley[12] in Pakistan, there were boats on the river from about 3300 BCE. The boats carried people and food and many other things, like gold, silver, and pots.

[11] **human:** about people

[12] **valley:** low ground between hills or mountains, often with a river going through it

A pot from the Indus Valley

The people in the Indus Valley made their boats out of plants from the river called reeds. These boats were very strong. They could travel on the **ocean**. People in India and Pakistan still use these boats today.

Like rivers, **lakes** are good places for people to live. Lake Titicaca is a very big lake in South America. Part of the lake is in Peru and part of it is in Bolivia. It is more than 3,000 meters above sea level. But those aren't the only interesting things about Lake Titicaca.

In the lake, there are more than 40 islands called *Islas Flotantes*. These are not regular islands. They are floating islands. The Uros people make them from thousands and thousands of reeds. They build these islands and live on them. The bigger islands have about ten Uros families. The smaller islands have only two or three families. Family life and the water from the lake slowly destroy the reeds, so the families have to add more reeds to their island every few months.

The Uros islands of Lake Titicaca

Niagara Falls

There are many other forms of water on the Earth. **Waterfalls** are beautiful. The name waterfall says it all – water falls from a high place to a lower place.

People love to visit waterfalls. Niagara Falls, between the USA and Canada, is a very popular place. Every year, about 14 million people visit there! Every second, an average of 2,407m^3 of water falls in Niagara. That's the same as 1,400 bathtubs full of water!

People also like to visit geysers. Water very far under the ground meets very hot rocks. The water gets hotter and hotter and finally boils.[13] Then it comes out of the ground very fast and flies high into the air as a geyser.

Old Faithful, a geyser in Yellowstone

[13]**boil:** when water goes up to the temperature of 99.98°C

There are more than 600 geysers in the world. About half of them are in Yellowstone National Park in Wyoming, United States.

In some parts of the world, there is very little water. There are no rivers or lakes, and there is very little rain. In other places, there is water but it is not clean.

In the world, there are 884 million people who don't have enough water to drink, to grow food, or to wash. Sometimes people have to walk for hours every day to get water. Some people are working to develop different ways to provide clean water in areas of the world without it.

Getting water from a well

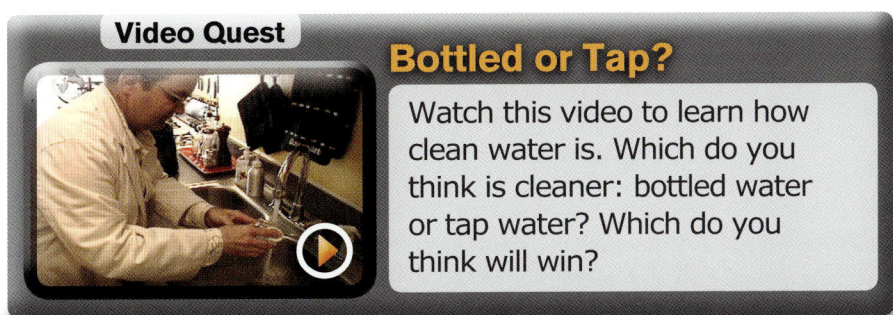

Video Quest

Bottled or Tap?

Watch this video to learn how clean water is. Which do you think is cleaner: bottled water or tap water? Which do you think will win?

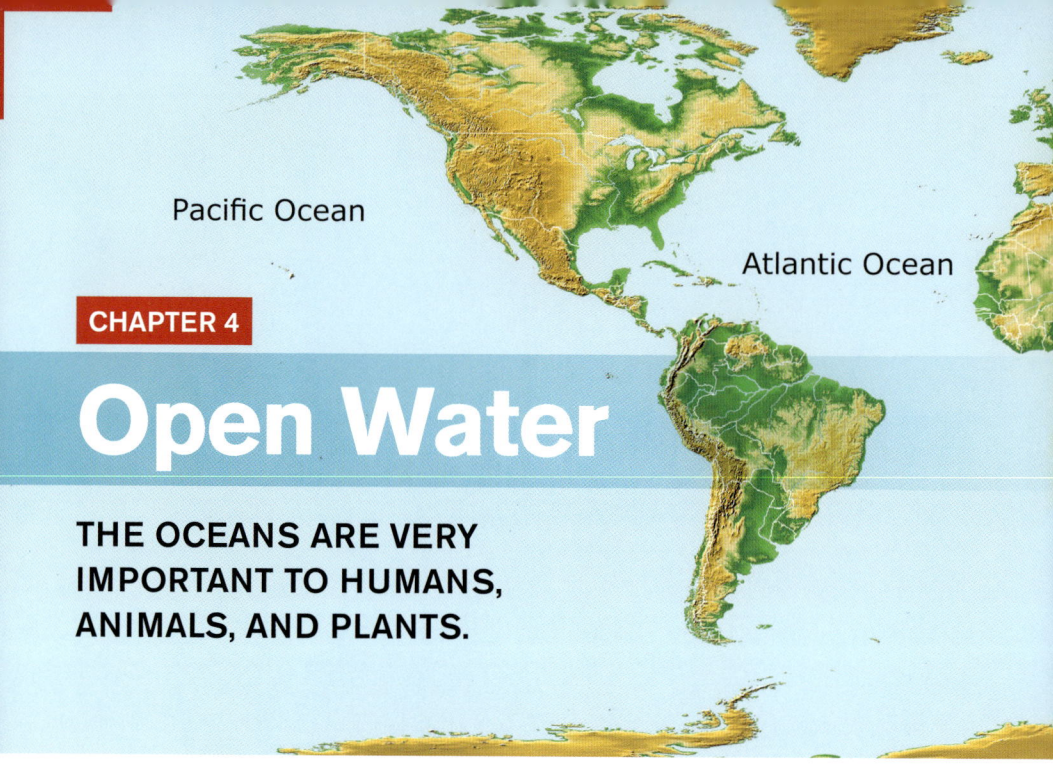

Pacific Ocean

Atlantic Ocean

CHAPTER 4

Open Water

THE OCEANS ARE VERY IMPORTANT TO HUMANS, ANIMALS, AND PLANTS.

The oceans and seas hold 97 percent of the Earth's water. They cover 71 percent of the Earth. All of this open water is salt water.

There are five oceans on Earth: the Atlantic, the Pacific, the Indian, the Arctic, and the Antarctic. The Pacific Ocean is the largest. It has 49.5 percent of the Earth's water. The Pacific Ocean also has the most kinds of plants and animals.

About 50 percent of all species[14] on Earth live in the oceans.

[14]**species:** a group of animals or plants that are the same

The oceans change the Earth's weather. When the temperature in some parts of the ocean is unusually warm, it is called El Niño. When the temperature is unusually cold, it is called La Niña. In Spanish, *niño* means "boy," and *niña* means "girl."

El Niño and La Niña change the weather, affecting[15] rain and wind. For example, during El Niño years, some parts of Australia and Indonesia don't get enough rain. During La Niña years, they get more rain than usual.

El Niño usually comes every three to seven years, but it is difficult to predict.[16] Nobody really knows when the next El Niño will come.

....

[15] **affect:** make changes in

[16] **predict:** say when something will happen in the future

A monsoon in the Indian Ocean

The way a body of water moves is called the current. Most ocean currents move in one direction[17] all the time. But, in the north part of the Indian Ocean, currents change direction twice a year. They change direction because of the **monsoon** winds.

From November to March, the cool, dry, northeast monsoon winds push the currents to Africa. In May, the winds come in the opposite direction, moving the water to India again. This change brings a lot of rain to India and other countries in Asia in a very short time.

Like floods, monsoons can be good or bad for people. The rain helps crops grow, but it can also destroy homes and businesses.

Most of the Earth's water is salt water. How salty is the ocean? Put one teaspoon of salt into a glass of water. Then drink a little. This is about the same as ocean water.

[17]**direction:** the way that someone or something is going

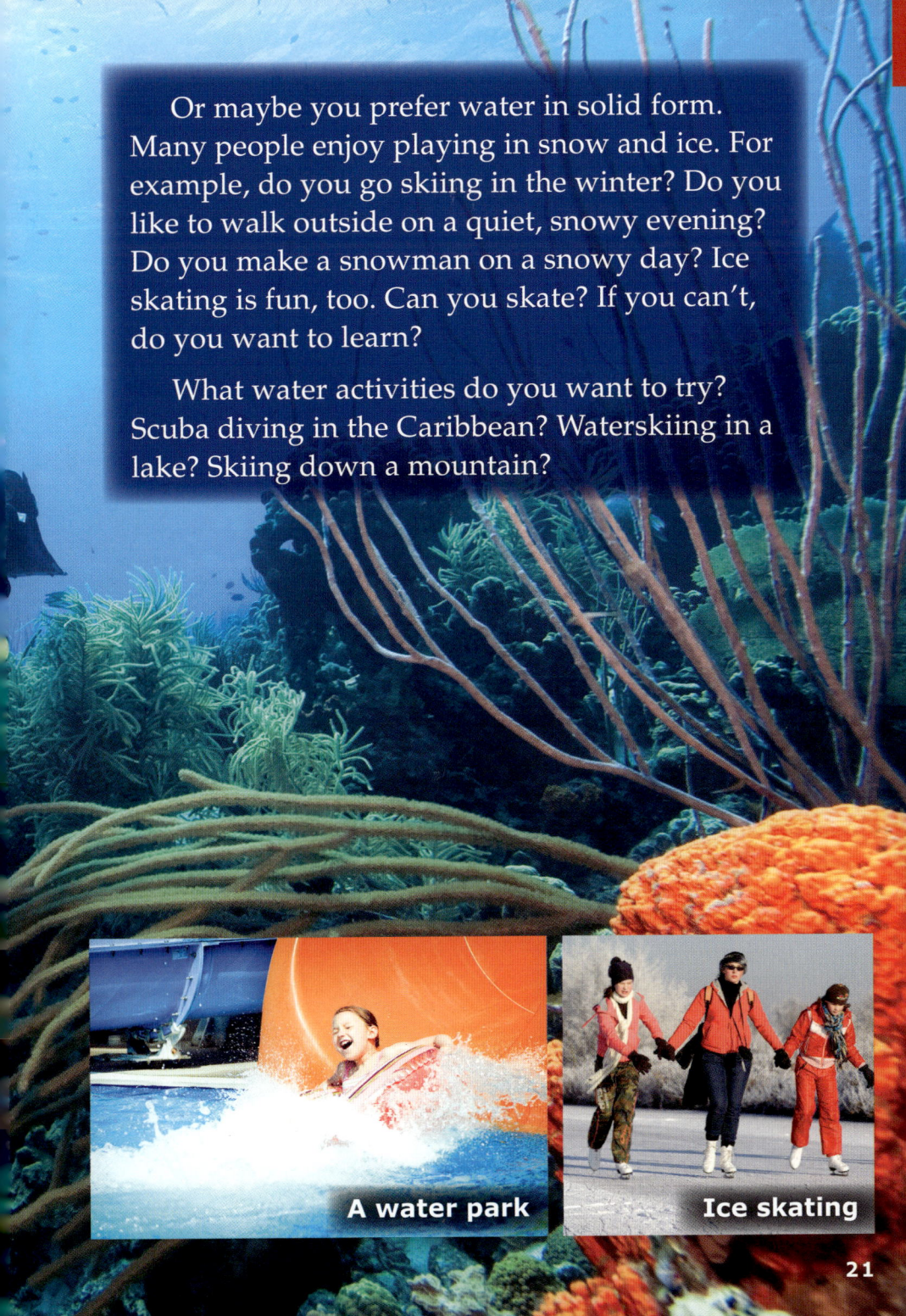

Or maybe you prefer water in solid form. Many people enjoy playing in snow and ice. For example, do you go skiing in the winter? Do you like to walk outside on a quiet, snowy evening? Do you make a snowman on a snowy day? Ice skating is fun, too. Can you skate? If you can't, do you want to learn?

What water activities do you want to try? Scuba diving in the Caribbean? Waterskiing in a lake? Skiing down a mountain?

A water park

Ice skating

After You Read

Read the sentences and choose Ⓐ (True) or Ⓑ (False).

1 People in medieval times used more water than people today.

Ⓐ True

Ⓑ False

2 The average person can live without food for about a month.

Ⓐ True

Ⓑ False

3 When a dog shakes, it moves all the parts of its body.

Ⓐ True

Ⓑ False

4 A cloud is a group of very tiny drops of water.

Ⓐ True

Ⓑ False

5 We get fog in hot weather.

Ⓐ True

Ⓑ False

6 High humidity makes the body feel colder.

Ⓐ True

Ⓑ False

7 People can make floating islands.

Ⓐ True

Ⓑ False

8 Icebergs are made of salt water.

Ⓐ True

Ⓑ False

Match

Match the vocabulary with the correct definitions.

Words	Definitions
① gas ___	a. very, very small
② tiny ___	b. how hot or cold something is
③ drop ___	c. people need it to live and breathe
④ air ___	d. you can drink water in this form
⑤ solid ___	e. you cannot see water in this form
⑥ temperature ___	f. one very small bit of water
⑦ liquid ___	g. having water on something
⑧ wet ___	h. change from ice to drinking water
⑨ melt ___	i. you can stand on water in this form

Answer the Questions

Read pages 14–19 again and answer the questions.

① Where is Niagara Falls?

_____

② What do you call a place where boiling water comes out of the ground quickly?

_____

③ Where is most of the Earth's fresh water?

_____

Answer Key

Words to Know, page 4

1 drops **2** wet **3** oceans **4** freeze

Words to Know, page 5

1 liquid **2** temperature **3** gas **4** solid **5** air **6** melts

Video Quest, page 5

They shake. They move their heads from side to side and the water flies off it.

Apply, page 9

Answers will vary.

Evaluate, page 11

Suggested Answer: They can kill people and destroy homes.

Video Quest, page 15

tap water

Video Quest, page 19

It begins its life as snow. It ends its life as part of the ocean.

True or False, page 22

1 B **2** A **3** B **4** A **5** B **6** B **7** A **8** B

Match, page 23

1 e **2** a **3** f **4** c **5** i **6** b **7** d **8** g **9** h

Answer the Questions, page 23

1 between the USA and Canada **2** geyser **3** glaciers